Sch

REVOLUTION!

THE EASTER RISING

Richard Killeen

Wayland

REVOLUTION!

1848 Year of Revolution
The American Revolution
The Easter Rising
The French Revolution
Revolution in Europe 1989
The Russian Revolution

Cover picture: *Members of the Irish Citizen Army on the rooftop of Liberty Hall.*
Title page picture: *A British machine-gun unit fires at the rebels.*

Book editor: Marcella Forster
Series editor: Paul Mason
Designer: Stonecastle Graphics Ltd

First published in 1995 by Wayland (Publishers) Ltd,
61 Western Road, Hove, East Sussex BN3 1JD, England

British Library Cataloguing in Publication Data
Killeen, Richard
Easter Rising. – (Revolution! Series)
I. Title II. Series
941.50821

ISBN 0-7502-1473-2

Typeset by Stonecastle Graphics Ltd, Marden, Tonbridge, Kent, England
Printed and bound by G. Canale & C.S.p.A., Turin, Italy

Picture acknowledgements

The publisher would like to thank
the following:
Mary Evans Picture Library:
14–15, 16 (bottom), 21, 26–27,
33 (top); Robert Harding Picture
Library/Paul Grundy: 45; Hulton
Deutsch: 6, 6–7, 7 (top), 8, 9, 13,
15, 18, 22 (top), 24 (bottom),
28–29, 29 (left), 32–33, 35, 38,
38–39, 42, 44–45; Illustrated
London News Picture Library:
cover, 5 (bottom), 10–11, 12,
22 (bottom); Irish National
Library: 10, 16 (top) 23, 29 (right),
31 (right), 34, 36, 39; the Mansell
Collection: 31 (left); Range/
Bettmann/UPI: title page, 30;
Popperfoto: 5 (top),
11 (bottom), 19, 24–25, 27 (top),
32 (top), 37, 40, 41, 43.
Maps were provided by Peter Bull.

CONTENTS

'THE GPO – CHARGE!'

Just before noon a group of about 150 men came out of Liberty Hall, Dublin. They lined up in ranks on the road outside, then marched in step towards Sackville Street, the main street in the city, just a few hundred yards away. They were heading for the General Post Office (GPO).

Some of the marchers wore uniform. About a quarter wore the dark-green uniform of the Irish Citizen Army. Others wore a different uniform, the grey-green of the Irish Volunteers.

The men were armed with an odd mixture of rifles, shotguns and handguns. They marched along in the sunshine, up an almost empty Sackville Street. It was a public holiday. The few people who watched the parade took little notice of it. Such sights had become quite common over the past three or four years. Various small

Below *This map of Dublin in 1916 shows the main locations of fighting during the Easter Rising.*

KEY
1   SOUTH DUBLIN UNION
2   FOUR COURTS
3   DUBLIN CASTLE
4   JACOB'S BISCUIT FACTORY
5   KINGSBRIDGE STATION
6   ROYAL COLLEGE OF SURGEONS
7   MENDICITY INSTITUTION
8   GENERAL POST OFFICE
9   LIBERTY HALL
10 ST STEPHENS GREEN
11 SHELBOURNE HOTEL
12 BOLAND'S MILLS
13 CLANWILLIAM HOUSE/MOUNT ST BRIDGE
14 BEGGAR'S BUSH BARRACKS
15 AMIENS ST STATION

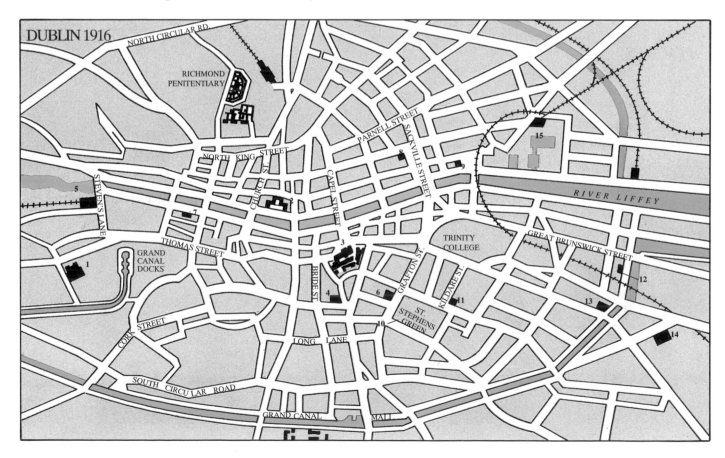

JAMES CONNOLLY

Born in Edinburgh, Scotland, of Irish parents, James Connolly was self-educated. As a young man he served in the British army. He became a socialist and trade union organizer. In 1896, aged twenty-eight, he went to Ireland to help foster the socialist movement there. He went to the United States in 1903 but was back in Ireland by 1910. Connolly became a leading figure in the Irish Transport and General Workers' Union (ITGWU) and helped found its own militia force, the Irish Citizen Army. He played a key role in the Great Dublin Lock-Out of 1913, one of the most important events in Irish trade union history. Eventually Connolly took over leadership of the ITGWU. He was convinced of the need for socialism and nationalism to march hand in hand and had himself planned a Citizen Army rising against British rule when the military council of the Irish Republican Brotherhood (IRB) let him in on their plans.

Sackville Street, Dublin. The rebels marched down this street, stormed the GPO (on the left) and established their headquarters there. This photograph was taken after the Rising.

groups had been playing at soldiers. Nobody took them seriously.

But this time it was different. When the men reached the GPO their leader, James Connolly, barked out, 'Halt. Left turn.' Then he gave the order: 'The GPO – charge!' The few armed guards on duty were taken completely by surprise. Not that it mattered – it later turned out that they had no ammunition for their guns!

PATRICK PEARSE

Patrick Pearse was the son of an English church sculptor who settled in Dublin and married an Irish woman. From an early age Pearse was devoted to the revival of the Irish language, and it became his life's cause. A gifted teacher, he opened his own boys' school. He was also a poet and a brilliant orator. Never a very practical man, Pearse was none the less appointed commander-in-chief of the rebel forces, although James Connolly ran things on a day-to-day basis once the fighting began. Along with Connolly, he was the principal author of the Proclamation of the Irish Republic.

Left Patrick Pearse, pictured shortly before the Easter Rising. Pearse liked to be photographed in profile because he had a cast in his left eye that he did not want people to see.

Right An IRB bomb exploded prematurely at London Bridge in 1884, killing the three IRB men who planted it. This was one of a series of attacks on England.

Below In 1880, Irish Catholics living in Glasgow rioted in protest at Protestants' opposition to home rule in Ireland. The riot sparked off the Catholic–Protestant rivalry that still exists today on the football field between Celtic and Rangers.

Once inside, the armed men took control of the building. They removed the British flag, the Union Jack, from the flagpole and ran up two different flags: a plain green flag with the words 'Irish Republic' and a green, white and orange tricolour. It was the first time that flag had flown over Dublin. Outside, on the steps, a man called Patrick Pearse began to read a statement: the Proclamation of the Irish Republic. A few onlookers listened without much interest.

Who were these men suddenly causing all this commotion in the centre of Dublin on a quiet Easter Monday? Many of them were not only Volunteers or members of the Citizen Army; they also belonged to a much older group, one of the most secret organizations in

Ireland. It was called the Irish Republican Brotherhood (IRB).

The IRB – sometimes called the Fenians – had been founded in 1858. It was a secret revolutionary group that conspired to overthrow British rule in Ireland by force – and only by force, for the IRB had no faith that politics or any other non-violent course of action could achieve what they wanted: an Irish republic, completely separate from Britain. The IRB had attempted a rebellion in 1867 but failed and had also been involved in terrorist dynamite attacks on English targets in the 1880s. Its followers were the most extreme Irish nationalists.

Until the early years of the twentieth century, the IRB had achieved little or nothing. In 1916, their policies were much less popular than those of the Home Rule Party and the organization was little more than a joke. Most people supported the Home Rule Party. Then a new generation of radicals joined the IRB and inherited control from the tired old men. They set about reviving the IRB's fortunes, and did so with such success that within ten years they had organized the Easter Rising.

THE HOME RULE PARTY

Home Rulers wanted Ireland to have its own parliament to decide its home affairs within the UK. At the time of the Easter Rising, the Home Rule Party had around eighty seats in the British parliament.

Home rule had been the main Irish demand since the 1870s. At last, in 1912, the Home Rulers seemed to have succeeded. A Home Rule act that would grant Ireland control of many of its own domestic affairs passed through the British parliament. However, by the time it finally completed its journey through parliament, it was the summer of 1914. On 4 August that year Britain entered the First World War, and the establishment of Irish Home Rule was suspended until the end of the fighting.

THOMAS J. CLARKE

Tom Clarke was one of the hard-liners of the IRB. He was also the oldest of the 1916 leaders. Born in 1857, he had been involved in one of the dynamite campaigns in England in the 1880s, for which he served fifteen years in prison. Clarke was a hero to the young radicals. At the insistence of the other leaders, he was the first person to sign the Proclamation of the Irish Republic.

The two most important people in the revived IRB were Thomas J. Clarke and Sean MacDermott. Clarke was a veteran of the IRB's dynamite campaign in England in the 1880s. MacDermott, a generation younger than Clarke, was a born organizer and conspirator. Both had a burning belief in the need for a rising to establish a separate Irish republic. For them, mere home rule was useless.

Many IRB members – including Clarke and MacDermott – occupied leading positions in the Irish Volunteers, maintaining the IRB's secret command structure within the Volunteers. Clarke and MacDermott began to plot a rising, deciding to try to use the Volunteers to carry out the IRB's plans to overthrow British rule in Ireland.

So secret was the conspiracy that even some leaders of the IRB, never mind the Volunteers, were kept in the dark. Right up to Easter week, some of the leading IRB men were deceived. This 'military council' was, therefore, a secret minority within the IRB, and the IRB was a secret minority within the Volunteers. It was a small, tight group. It included Joseph Plunkett, the main military planner, and Patrick Pearse. Most importantly, James Connolly was taken into the IRB's confidence.

THE IRISH VOLUNTEERS

The Irish Volunteers were formed in Dublin in late 1913. They were a nationalist militia pledged to support the enforcement of home rule. When the First World War broke out, John Redmond, leader of the Home Rule party, called on the Volunteers to enrol in the British army. The vast majority of the 180,000 members answered his call, changing their name to the National Volunteers. The remaining 10,000 or so kept their old name, the Irish Volunteers, and refused to fight for Britain, promising to resist any effort to introduce conscription in Ireland.

Irish Volunteers – woefully short of arms – parade in Dublin in May 1914. Later the organization split over whether or not to support the British in the First World War.

James Connolly was the leader of the Irish Transport and General Workers' Union. His tiny militia, the Irish Citizen Army, numbered no more than 200 men but – incredible though it seems – he was proposing a rising of his own! The IRB joined forces with him rather than let him play the wild card. He was to prove the rebels' best commander in the field.

The military council's greatest need was for arms, for without them there was no chance of a rebellion at all. To get arms, the council used the services of one of the most unlikely of the Volunteers, Sir Roger Casement. A former employee of the British government's Foreign Office, he had been born in County Antrim and was a long-time Irish nationalist sympathizer. At the outbreak of the First World War, Casement went to Germany – Britain's enemy – and eventually arranged for the shipment of a cargo of arms to Ireland aboard a German ship, the *Aud*. It was due to arrive off the south-west coast of Ireland on Good Friday, 1916.

Despite the IRB's secrecy, the British authorities in Dublin Castle knew that something was going on, though

JOSEPH PLUNKETT

Joseph Plunkett, the son of a wealthy scholar who was also a papal count, was a poet and traveller. After some years abroad, he returned to Dublin in 1911 and became a well-known figure in literary circles. He also turned to politics and joined the IRB, being one of the most vigorous organizers of the rebellion. He used his knowledge of military strategy to draw up the plans for the occupation of Dublin's public buildings. However, Plunkett's health failed at the start of 1916, and by the time of the Easter Rising he was a dying man.

Above *British troops board an armoured train in County Clare on their way to fight the rebels in Dublin. Troops were carried to Dublin by rail from barracks all over Ireland.*

Right *Despite being a British Foreign Office employee, Sir Roger Casement was committed to Irish nationalism. He received his knighthood for exposing the abuse of human rights in Africa.*

they were not sure what exactly. Then came sensational news. The *Aud* had been intercepted by a Royal Navy ship! The *Aud*'s German master immediately scuttled his ship, and the IRB's arms shipment went to the bottom of the sea. Casement was captured from an accompanying German submarine. It seemed that the game was up. The British authorities relaxed.

The capture of the *Aud* surprised not only the British authorities at Dublin Castle but also the official leadership of the Volunteers and even some of the top people in the IRB itself, all of whom now realized that the military council had been deceiving them for months. With the arms gone, everyone assumed that the rising was off. The leader of the Volunteers, Eoin MacNeill, ordered that all Volunteer movements for the whole Easter weekend be cancelled. But the military council was determined. They had some arms, although fewer than they would have wished, and they were going to make a stand come what may. They met on Easter Sunday – the day the Rising was supposed to have broken out – and decided to go ahead

Right *Eoin MacNeill, leader of the Volunteers. This photograph was taken after the Rising, in 1923.*

Below *Members of the Irish Citizen Army on the rooftop of Liberty Hall shortly before the Easter Rising.*

TIMELINE
Easter Monday, 24 April

10 am – noon
The Irish Volunteers start to gather at Liberty Hall, Dublin, and are dispatched to various garrisons around the city.

11.45 am
The first shots of the rising are fired at the British authorities in Dublin Castle. The rebels miss their chance to capture it and withdraw instead to nearby City Hall.

Noon
The main group of Volunteers march from Liberty Hall and take over the GPO.

1 pm
The tricolour flag is raised over the GPO. Patrick Pearse reads the Proclamation of the Irish Republic.

Afternoon
The Volunteers inside the GPO fortify their garrison and surround it with barricades.

Late afternoon
British troops arrive from the Curragh. After a brief fight, the British recapture City Hall. Rebels hold out at Mendicity Institution.

the next morning. They knew that MacNeill's orders would keep most Volunteers at home, but they expected enough people to turn out to make a show.

It was these people, the secret military council of the IRB, who led the charge on Dublin's GPO that Easter Monday morning. Meanwhile, other small groups established themselves in six other locations around the city centre. The Easter Rising was on.

Once inside the GPO, the military council sandbagged and fortified their garrison against the expected British counter-attack. Barricades were set up in the surrounding streets and snipers moved into position at nearby vantage points.

TIMELINE
The Build-up to the Easter Rising

1858
Foundation of the Irish Republican Brotherhood (IRB), also known as the Fenians.

1867
Unsuccessful rebellion against the British authorities in Ireland.

1883
Tom Clarke sent to jail for bombing offences.

1886
The first Home Rule bill fails.

1907
Tom Clarke returns to Ireland.
The revival of the IRB.

1912
The third Home Rule bill passes through the House of Commons.

1913
The foundation of the Irish Volunteers.

1914
The outbreak of the First World War.
The Home Rule bill is finally passed by the House of Lords but its implementation is suspended until the end of the war.

1915
Roger Casement goes to Germany and arranges an arms shipment to Ireland for the military council.

1916
January   The military council drafts a final plan for the Easter Rising.
Connolly's Irish Citizen Army joins the plot.

April 21   The arms shipment is discovered by the British navy.
Roger Casement is captured.

April 22   Eoin MacNeill orders the Irish Volunteers not to mobilize.

April 24   Easter Monday. The Rising goes ahead in Dublin.

Above *Captain William Redmond leads a parade of National Volunteers. He was the brother of John Redmond, the Home Rule leader, and was killed in action on the Western Front in 1917.*

On the far side of the river from the GPO was Dublin Castle, the headquarters of the British authorities. Just before noon on Easter Monday, a small group from the Citizen Army attacked the castle, firing the first shots of the Rising. They quickly captured the six soldiers in the guardhouse but then did not press on. They probably found it difficult to believe that Dublin Castle – for centuries the centre of British government in Ireland – was at their mercy. But it was: there were barely twenty-five soldiers and two officers in the whole place.

Had the Castle been captured, it would have been a major victory. However, the chance was missed and instead the rebels moved on to occupy nearby City Hall.

> 'When I reached the top floor [of the GPO] O'Rahilly came forward. Still smiling. "They were determined to have a rising," he said, "so here we are."
>
> ' "How long do you think that we can last?" I asked.
>
> ' "By a miracle we might last for 24 hours," he replied, "but I don't think we'll go for that long."
>
> 'I thought his estimate extremely optimistic.'
>
> – From the memoirs of Desmond Fitzgerald, a member of the Volunteers who later became a cabinet minister in the first independent government of Ireland.

Dublin Castle was for centuries the symbol of British rule in Ireland.

THE BRITISH RESPOND

The counter-attack began on Tuesday morning. Troops under the command of General W. H. M. Lowe had arrived from the Curragh – about thirty-five miles away – on Monday evening and began taking up their positions on Tuesday morning. They threw a cordon across Dublin from west to east, bringing them into immediate conflict with rebels in the Mendicity Institution. A bitter battle raged for three days.

In St Stephen's Green, a large square with a central park in the fashionable south side of Dublin, a Citizen Army group under the command of Michael Mallin and the exotic Countess Constance Markievicz dug themselves in. They had originally hoped to occupy the Shelbourne Hotel, the tallest building around the Green, but they did not have enough troops to hold such a large building. When the British arrived, they fell back to the College of Surgeons – a much lower building – and the Shelbourne was promptly occupied by a British machine-gun crew.

Michael Mallin, a Dubliner, led the Irish Citizen Army troops at the College of Surgeons garrison. He had served in the British army for fourteen years, starting as a drummer boy and leaving as a non-commissioned officer. He then worked as a silk weaver and became a trade unionist.

COUNTESS CONSTANCE MARKIEVICZ

Countess Markievicz was the highest-ranking woman among the rebel forces and one of the most extraordinary women in Ireland – or anywhere else. Born into a rich Anglo-Irish family in County Sligo in 1868, she was presented at court to Queen Victoria at the age of nineteen as 'the new Irish beauty'. She studied art in London and Paris, drifted into radical political circles, married a Polish-Ukrainian count and returned to Dublin in 1903. She soon took up Irish causes: the Irish language, nationalism and socialism.

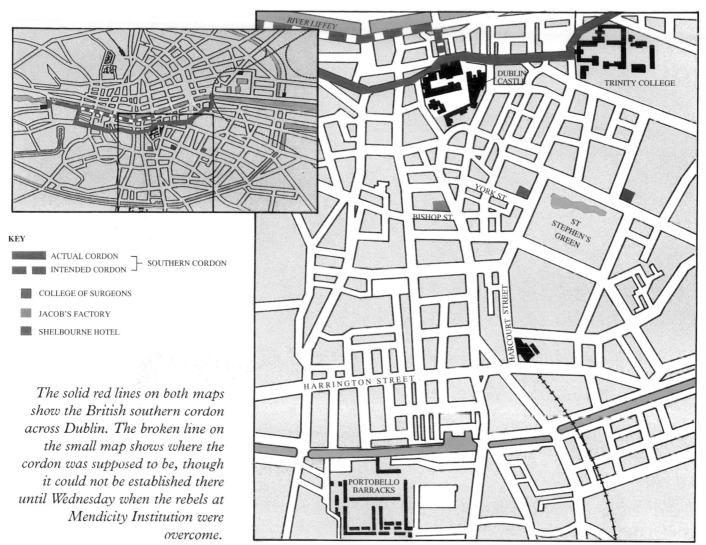

ACTUAL CORDON
INTENDED CORDON — SOUTHERN CORDON

COLLEGE OF SURGEONS

JACOB'S FACTORY

SHELBOURNE HOTEL

The solid red lines on both maps show the British southern cordon across Dublin. The broken line on the small map shows where the cordon was supposed to be, though it could not be established there until Wednesday when the rebels at Mendicity Institution were overcome.

'The rain was falling now persistently, and persistently from the Green and from the Shelbourne Hotel snipers were exchanging bullets. Some distance beyond the Shelbourne I saw another volunteer stretched out on a seat just within the railings. He wasn't dead for, now and again, his hand moved feebly in a gesture for aid. The hand was completely red with blood. His face could not be seen. He was just a limp mass upon which the rain beat pitilessly and he was sodden and shapeless, and most miserable to see. His companions could not draw him in for the spot was covered by the snipers from the Shelbourne. Bystanders stated several attempts had already been made to rescue him but that he would have to remain there until the fall of night.' – From James Stephens's diary of Easter week, *Insurrection in Dublin*.

The machine-gunners soon established a series of gun placements on the fourth floor of the Shelbourne Hotel. From there they had a clear aim at the College of Surgeons. A deadly hail of fire soon hit those rebels still in the park. Five of them were killed before the rest succeeded in retreating across the street to the relative safety of the college. By 7 am the entire St Stephen's Green garrison, consisting of about 100 men, women and boys, had retreated to the College of Surgeons. They were safe for the moment, but their position was obviously hopeless.

Around the city, other rebel commands maintained as much pressure as they could on nearby British troops. It was mainly a question of sniping from whatever vantage points they could secure, but it was enough to keep the British in a state of nervous alert.

By now it was clear that the confusion prior to the Rising was taking its toll. Eoin MacNeill's orders cancelling all Volunteer activity had two effects. First, and most obviously, the number of people that actually turned out to fight was much lower than had been planned; second, there was no national uprising. Dublin was virtually on its own.

One of the Volunteers inside the GPO, Desmond Fitzgerald, left this record of his conversations with Patrick Pearse in the first few days of the Rising: *'Time and time again we came back to one favourite topic which could not be avoided. And that was the moral rectitude [rightness] of what we had undertaken . . . We each brought forward every . . . argument and quotation that could justify the Rising.'*

Left *Carts, baskets and a car were used to make this street barricade on the west side of St Stephen's Green, just outside the College of Surgeons.*

THOMAS MACDONAGH

Thomas MacDonagh, born in 1878, was an Irish-language enthusiast. He taught with Pearse and from there went on to University College, Dublin, where he was a lecturer in the department of English literature. A poet and essayist, MacDonagh was also a member of the IRB. He was one of the military council who planned the Easter Rising, during which he commanded the Jacob's Factory garrison.

Above *A British soldier captured by the rebels during the Rising is led away by a Dublin policeman at the end of the fighting. Prisoners were held captive in the GPO garrison.*

By nightfall of the second day of the Rising, General Lowe had about 5,000 troops at his disposal, vastly outnumbering the rebels. In the afternoon four artillery pieces had arrived, and Lowe was beginning the work of throwing a cordon around the northern suburbs which, together with the southern cordon established earlier, would trap the rebels' GPO and Four Courts garrisons.

TIMELINE
Tuesday, 25 April

4–5 am
British troops march up Kildare Street and occupy the Shelbourne Hotel, establishing a machine-gun post on the fourth floor.

5–7 am
British troops attack the Citizen Army contingent dug in at the park on St Stephen's Green, killing five rebels.

7 am
The Citizen Army contingent retreats to the garrison at the College of Surgeons.

Noon
The British troops complete a cordon from Kingsbridge Station to College Green.

Afternoon
The first attack on the South Dublin Union garrison.

The positions of rebel garrisons and the British cordons. The northern cordon was intended to run along North King Street but never did, thanks to the rebels.

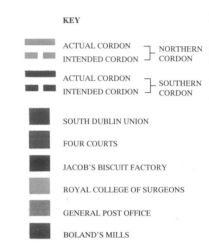

KEY

ACTUAL CORDON
INTENDED CORDON } NORTHERN CORDON

ACTUAL CORDON
INTENDED CORDON } SOUTHERN CORDON

SOUTH DUBLIN UNION

FOUR COURTS

JACOB'S BISCUIT FACTORY

ROYAL COLLEGE OF SURGEONS

GENERAL POST OFFICE

BOLAND'S MILLS

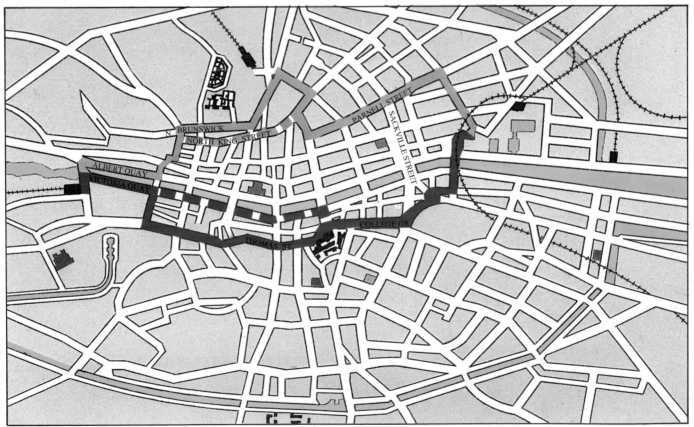

Wednesday, 26 April

THE ARRIVAL OF THE 'HELGA'

Just before 8 am on Wednesday morning a small, grey fisheries patrol boat sailed up the River Liffey and tied up on the south quays, opposite the Custom House. It was the *Helga*, sent there by the British to shell the rebel positions. The *Helga's* first target was Liberty Hall, just across the narrow river. The British wrongly thought that it was still full of rebels. In fact, it was empty except for the caretaker, Peter Ennis.

Liberty Hall was shelled by the Helga, *but the building was empty except for the caretaker, who escaped by the skin of his teeth.*

British snipers, waiting on nearby buildings to shoot Citizen Army men fleeing from Liberty Hall, found no target other than poor Peter Ennis, the caretaker – and sole occupant of the hall. John O'Leary, a reporter, watched as Ennis fled for his life: *'A machine-gun is turned on him. Bullets hit the pavement in front of him and behind him, they strike the roadway and the walls of the building along his route and still he runs on and on. I hold my breath in awe as I watch his mad career. Will he escape? He will . . . he won't. "My God!" I exclaim as a bullet raises a spark from the pavement right at his toe. A hundred yards in nine seconds – a record! Nonsense, this man does the distance in five and disappears, his breath in his fist, his heart in his mouth but – safe!'*

EAMON DE VALERA

De Valera was the son of a Spanish father and an Irish mother. He grew up in County Limerick. A teacher of mathematics and an Irish language enthusiast, he commanded the Boland's Mills garrison during the Rising.

Above *Eamon de Valera dominated Irish politics for the first half of the twentieth century. This photograph was taken about ten years after the Rising.*

The first shell was fired at exactly 8 am. Instead of flying across the river, it hit the Loop Line railway bridge with a noisy clatter that was heard all over Dublin. The crew of the *Helga* adjusted their gun sights and fired again. This time they were spot on: the shell vaulted over the river and exploded on the roof of Liberty Hall, leaving only the outer walls intact.

Soon the British troops had established a clear line of fire into rebel-held Lower Sackville Street. Lowe wanted to capture the central rebel position at the GPO first of all.

While the attack was being prepared, one of the most tragic incidents of the Rising was taking place across the city in Portobello Barracks. One of the best-known characters in Dublin, Francis Sheehy-Skeffington, had been arrested the night before as he was walking home. Skeffington was no threat to public order; in fact he was a pacifist. Earlier in the day he had stood in Sackville Street, armed with nothing more than a walking stick, and tried to stop a mob from the nearby tenements looting shops. He was shot in cold blood on the orders of Captain J. C. Bowen-Colthurst of the Royal Irish Rifles. He was the most innocent victim of Easter week. Colthurst was mad, and his insanity claimed three other lives apart from Skeffington's.

Left *British troops man a barricade in a side street off Sackville Street.*

At this stage, however, the fighting centred on the Mendicity Institution. The Volunteer commander, Sean Heuston, had barely twenty men at his disposal, most of them in their early twenties. They had inflicted over a hundred casualties on the British forces, but now they were surrounded on all sides. Behind them, the rising ground offered ideal positions for British snipers. A constant stream of fire came at them from across the River Liffey. Finally, hand grenades were lobbed into the building; by noon Heuston decided to surrender.

Having finished its work at Liberty Hall, the *Helga* sailed down the Liffey to shell the rear of the Boland's Mills garrison. The mills lay along the railway line to Kingstown, the city's main port of entry and most likely means of bringing troops from Britain into Dublin. The commander of the Boland's Mills garrison, Eamon de Valera, ran a nationalist flag up the flagpole of a disused distillery nearby, and the *Helga* blazed away at the empty building, doing little damage to the Volunteers' position.

Meanwhile, out at Kingstown, British troops were landing. They were all to march to the Royal Hospital at the western end of the city centre, a journey of about nine miles. They split into three groups, two of which reached their destination safely. The third followed a route through the suburb of Ballsbridge – and straight into the teeth of the Volunteer position at Mount Street Bridge.

The fighting started at midday and went on until late in the evening. The British lost over two hundred men; the first volley alone claimed ten lives. These casualties were inflicted by only twelve Volunteers, four of whom survived. The whole affair was a triumph for the morale of the rebels and a disaster for the British.

That same afternoon, the GPO garrison came under a non-stop hail of British machine-gun fire, supported for the first time by artillery. The day had started with the shells from the *Helga*; it was ending with the boom of artillery.

'I could not look at Pearse's face without being moved. Its natural gravity now conveyed a sense of great tragedy. There was no doubt in my mind that when he looked round at the men and the girls there, he was convinced that they must all perish in the Rising to which he had brought them.'
– From the memoirs of Desmond Fitzgerald.

Below *British troops suffered heavy losses at Mount Street Bridge. They marched straight into a deadly hail of fire from the Volunteers in Clanwilliam House (on the left).*

Above *These British troops behind a Talbot Street barricade were in good spirits. Their position was out of range of the rebel garrisons.*

8 am
The *Helga* attacks Liberty Hall.

10.30 am
The murder of Francis Sheehy-Skeffington and two others in Portobello Barracks.

Noon
The evacuation of the Mendicity Institution by remaining volunteers under Sean Heuston. They rejoin the main garrison across the river in the Four Courts.

Early afternoon
The *Helga* sails down the River Liffey and begins to shell the rear of the Boland's Mills garrison.

2.30 pm
British reinforcements marching in from Kingstown meet the outpost of Boland's Mills garrison at Mount Street Bridge. Fierce fighting rages all afternoon, leaving over 200 British dead by evening.

4 pm
The first British artillery attack on the GPO garrison.

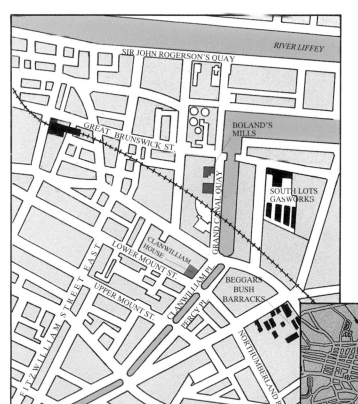

British troops marched straight into the jaws of rebel troops at Clanwilliam House in the Mount Street Bridge area.

Thursday, 27 April

BATTLES RAGE

This was the day on which Sackville Street burned. At exactly 10 am a non-stop artillery attack began. By the end of the day the lower part of the street was in flames.

Inside the GPO the heat from the flames outside was so intense that the rebels had to hose down the sacking on the barricaded windows for fear that it would catch fire.

The defenders – most of them Dubliners – watched the destruction of their city outside with a mixture of pride and horror. At times the flames shot hundreds of feet into the air.

At 10 pm, twelve hours into the bombardment, an oil works directly opposite the GPO caught fire, setting off a terrifying series of explosions. The rebels truly felt they might all be burned to death. As sparks began to hit the GPO roof, they moved all their bombs and other explosives to the basement.

Right *Sackville Street burns.*

Below *Soldiers sift through the ruins of a pub destroyed in the rebellion.*

Joseph Plunkett, who had spent most of the week lying on a mattress, too weakened by the tuberculosis that was killing him to take any active part in the fighting, looked at the scene and said, *'It's the first time it's happened since Moscow – the first time a capital has been burned since then.'*

As the flames consumed Lower Sackville Street and buildings crashed to the ground on that Thursday, Patrick Pearse defended the rebels' actions: *'Well, when we're all wiped out, people will blame us for everything, I suppose, and condemn us. Yet if it hadn't been for this protest, the [First World] War would have ended and nothing would have been done. After a few years people will see the meaning of what we tried to do.'*

The leaders of the rebellion knew that their position was utterly hopeless and that surrender was only a matter of time. They had known the whole rebellion to be hopeless from the start. As they had marched on Easter Monday morning, James Connolly had remarked to a colleague, 'We are going out to be slaughtered.' Yet they decided to press on. Why?

All the leaders believed in the need for an armed rebellion. It had been a fixed principle of the IRB since its foundation almost sixty years earlier. They believed that a nation needed to assert its independence through force in order to keep its self-respect. National honour demanded it. If that protest could only be a gesture – a symbol – then that was a pity, but it was no reason not to fight.

All that the rebels could do was delay the inevitable end for as long as possible and put up the best fight they could. In the middle of the afternoon, James Connolly was still full of energy. He directed the operations of the GPO in a brisk, no-nonsense way. The other leaders were in the background. Pearse spent most of the week drafting proclamations and bulletins; he had no talent for soldiering. Clarke and MacDermott took no leading role; they had nursed the conspiracy that set up the Rising and their work was done. Plunkett was in the last stages of a fatal illness. The other two signatories of the Proclamation of the Republic, Thomas MacDonagh and Eamonn Ceannt, were in charge of the Volunteer garrisons at the Jacob's factory and the South Dublin Union respectively.

Disaster struck when, on Thursday afternoon, Connolly was seriously wounded. He went out with a group of men from the GPO to set up a position in nearby Middle Abbey Street. The intention was to delay any British advance up that street, which joined Sackville Street just one block south of the GPO. The position was secured, but just as Connolly was about to return to the

TIMELINE
Irish rebellions against British rule

1798
The great rebellion of that summer claimed over 30,000 lives and led directly to the abolition of the old Irish parliament and of Ireland joining Britain fully under the Act of Union.

1803
Robert Emmet's rebellion was a serious conspiracy but a premature explosion in an arms dump alerted the authorities to it, and in the end it amounted to little more than a street brawl in Dublin.

1848
The Young Ireland rebellion, in which a small group of men caused a brief affray in County Tipperary, was also a failure.

1867
The Fenian (IRB) uprising was dogged by poor planning, ill luck and bad weather. It was put down without much difficulty by government forces.

Left *The Jacob's factory garrison, under the command of Thomas MacDonagh, was the most impenetrable rebel position and saw little action after the Tuesday of the Rising.*

Below *Eamonn Ceannt led the Volunteers at the South Dublin Union. He was originally from Galway and worked as a clerk for the treasury at Dublin Corporation.*

EAMONN CEANNT

Eamonn Ceannt was an enthusiast for the Irish language and traditional Irish music. He was a leading member of the Irish Volunteers from their foundation and led the South Dublin Union garrison during the Easter Rising.

Robert Emmet led the 1803 Irish rebellion against British rule and was a hero of Irish nationalism.

GPO a bullet ricocheted and hit him above the ankle. There was nothing for it but to crawl back to the GPO. In great pain and losing blood all the time, he made it. He was greatly weakened by his injury and the pain was intense. Connolly was not the same commanding figure for the rest of the Rising.

That same afternoon, a furious gun battle took place at the South Dublin Union between British troops and the Volunteer garrison under the command of Eamonn Ceannt and his tough little second-in-command, Cathal Brugha. It was unlike any other action seen all week. The British tried to recapture buildings in the sprawling complex and ended up in a cat-and-mouse chase from building to building. No one knew exactly where the enemy was. Were they up the next stairs? Or in that room? Or down that corridor? In fact, each side thought that the other was stronger than it actually was. Brugha was horribly wounded but survived. In the evening, just as the Volunteers expected the British to make a final assault, nothing happened.

Right A British machine-gun placement, flanked by riflemen, on a South Dublin Street. The rebels had no machine guns or artillery.

Right A British soldier crawls over Mount Street Bridge towards a sniper stronghold.

FIGHTING AT THE SOUTH DUBLIN UNION

This memoir was left by British Captain John Oates of the 2/8 Sherwood Foresters:

'[Captain] Martyn and Sergeant Walker were stretched flat on the floor just under the barricade with the [rebel] rifles sticking out of the barricade just over their heads. The rebels, apparently, were unable to depress them to the right angle. I saw Walker take the pin out of a bomb and try to throw it over from where he lay. Unfortunately there were only a few inches of space between the top of the barricade and the ornamental arch and it wasn't an easy thing to do. Instead of going over the bomb hit the top of the barricade and fell back into the room. I thought, "My God, that's the end of them." '

Incredibly, they survived.

Above *Cathal Brugha was second-in-command at the South Dublin Union garrison. He was born Charles Burgess but as a young man he adopted the Gaelic form of his name.*

TIMELINE
Thursday, 27 April

10 am
The beginning of continuous artillery barrage on Sackville Street by the British.

Mid-afternoon
James Connolly is wounded in Middle Abbey Street and struggles back to the GPO.

Afternoon
Ferocious fighting at South Dublin Union ends in stalemate.

The British, not realizing that the Volunteers were on their last legs, withdrew and from that moment on the South Dublin Union garrison was left alone. It saw no more action and was one of the last to surrender.

Friday, 28 April

THE GPO BURNS

On this Friday morning, James Connolly was placed on a stretcher and carried into the great public office of the GPO. He was still in pain, but he wished to stay at the heart of things. He remained, in Pearse's words, 'the guiding brain' of the Rising.

British troops brew tea under the Loop Line railway bridge, the ruins of Liberty Hall behind them. By now this area was safe for them.

Connolly called his secretary, Winifred Carney, and dictated a long address to the troops under his command. It was, on the face of it, crazy. It claimed that the rebels were winning when it was obvious that they were not. It claimed that the whole country was up in arms when it was quiet. It claimed that armed Volunteers were marching on Dublin from the provinces when there were no marching men.

Unlike Pearse, Connolly was no dreamer. This address to the troops had a purpose behind its seemingly empty boasting. The whole Rising was, after all, only a gesture. But the longer the gesture went on and the longer Irish patriots were seen to be fighting the might of the British Empire for their beliefs, the greater the rebels' chance of winning the hearts and minds of the Irish people. That was the point: to convince Irish people that the country's honour had been saved by the men of 1916.

This was the fifth day on which the tricolour of the republic was flying over public buildings in the Irish capital. It was the fifth day of armed resistance to defend that republic and that flag. Connolly wanted as much time as possible to get his message into people's minds: that

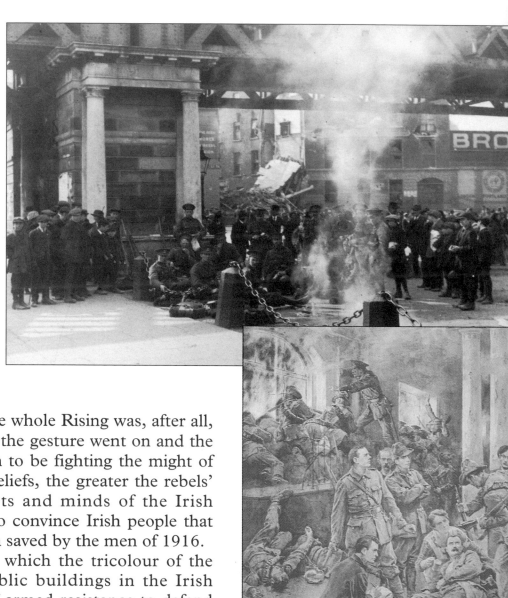

Reporter John O'Leary watched the last moments of the GPO: *'High above the doomed building, the Republican flag flutters in the stifling atmosphere of smoke . . . With my field-glasses, I can see the letters IRISH REPUBLIC scorch to a deep brown. Now and then the flag is buried as thousands of fragments of burning paper belch up as it were from a volcano. Now it begins to hang its head as if in shame. At 9 pm the GPO is in ruins, its granite walls look like the bones of a skeleton skull . . . The fluttering of the flag grows feebler. In the dimness of the night I see it give an occasional flutter, as if revived by a gust of air. At length at 9.51 pm the staff supporting it begins to waver and in a second falls out towards the street. The . . . fortress is no more.'*

Right At 4 pm the GPO roof caught fire. By 9 pm it was a burning ruin.

Below James Connolly lies wounded on a stretcher in the GPO. The bareheaded man standing to the left of him is Patrick Pearse.

total separation from Britain was not just a fantasy; it was a serious business. It was the work of serious people who were fighting a good fight.

And with every hour that the rebels could hold out, Connolly's message was getting through. All Irish nationalists disliked British rule in Ireland, and the sight of Irish men and women fighting British troops under an Irish flag was something to stir the emotions. Mixed with the horror was a tiny surge of pride. The Volunteers might be mad, but their hearts were in the right place.

By 4 pm on Friday the roof of the GPO was on fire. By the evening the building was an inferno. The Volunteers were forced to evacuate it and to retreat into surrounding buildings. Pearse and Connolly were the last to leave.

THE O'RAHILLY

Michael Joseph O'Rahilly assumed the title of a Gaelic clan chief. He was a journalist and, like so many of the men of 1916, an Irish language enthusiast. He was a member of the Irish Volunteers but was quite unaware of the secret IRB faction who were plotting the Rising. When their plans became known, he supported Eoin MacNeill and spent all of Easter Sunday night driving around the midlands delivering MacNeill's orders to stay at home to Volunteer units. Yet when he returned to Dublin and realized that the Rising was going to proceed anyway, even though on a small scale, he felt that in all honour he should join it. He fought with great gallantry, and was particularly concerned to see that no harm was done to those held prisoner by the GPO garrison. He died with the utmost courage while leading a breakout from the burning GPO. Years later, W. B. Yeats wrote a ballad about him:

'Am I such a craven that
I should not get the word
But for what some travelling man
Had heard I had not heard?'
Then on Pearse and Connolly
He fixed a bitter look
'Because I helped to wind the clock
I come to hear it strike.'

As the GPO was burning, the last and most savage action of the Rising was taking place barely half a mile away in North King Street.

The rebels were well dug into sniping positions, and they had a strong barricade thrown across North King Street. In theory General Lowe's cordon ran along that street. He realized that it would require cautious tactics to root out the rebels. But Lowe was no longer in charge. The British had sent a military supremo to Ireland. General Sir John Maxwell was a forceful man, and he ordered a frontal attack on the North King Street rebels.

Right *Poor children take timber from the ruins of buildings destroyed during the Rising. Looting was widespread during Easter week, much to the horror of some of the rebel leaders, who believed restraint was in order.*

'Written after I was shot – darling Nancy, I was shot leading a rush up Moore Street and took refuge in a doorway.

'While I was there I heard the men pointing out where I was and made a bolt for the laneway I am in now.

'I got more than one bullet I think. Tons and tons of love dearie to you and the boys and to Nell and Anna. It was a good fight anyhow. Please deliver this to Nancy O'Rahilly, 40 Herbert Park, Dublin. Goodbye darling.' – A final message from The O'Rahilly to his wife, Nancy. It was found on his body.

The result was a bloody street battle that lasted from just before 6 pm on Friday until Saturday morning. It was centred on Reilly's Fort, an empty public house. It overlooked and protected the rebels' barricade and gave them a clear view of the advancing British.

The British troops sent in to storm this position had been among those mauled at Mount Street Bridge on Wednesday. They were tough men of the South Staffordshire Regiment, but they were not used to this sort of fighting. They were nervous in this strange city where the enemy did not always wear uniform, where civilians soon were suspected of aiding the rebels, where unseen snipers could end your life at any moment.

All that – plus the fact that in over six hours' fighting in North King Street the South Staffs had by midnight nothing to show for their casualties – caused some of them to crack. They broke into the surrounding slum houses and took it out on civilians. By the time they were finished, fifteen innocent men had been murdered.

Above *General Sir John Maxwell, the British military supremo.*

Left *On Friday night there was bitter fighting in North King Street and at Reilly's Fort.*

KEY

ACTUAL NORTHERN CORDON

INTENDED NORTHERN CORDON

An eyewitness account by Mrs Ellen Walsh, a resident of North King Street, of one of the North King Street murders:

'We heard the soldiers banging at the street door . . . About thirty soldiers . . . ran at us like infuriated wild beasts or like things possessed. They looked ghastly and seemed in a panic. There was terrible firing going on outside in the street . . . The man in command shouted "Search them" and they searched the two men and the two boys. One of our men said: "There was no one firing from this house." . . . The women and children were then all ordered down into the back kitchen and my poor husband and Mr Hughes were brought upstairs . . . I shall never forget the horror of it. Sometime after I heard a voice upstairs crying "Mercy! Mercy! Don't put that on me!" and someone resisting as if being tied up, or having his eyes bandaged. The old man in the upper room close by heard my husband crying, and as they killed him he heard his last words: "O, Nellie, Nellie, jewel!"'

British troops use a tank to batter down the door of a house during their search for snipers.

It took a terrifying night of fighting before the small garrison at Reilly's Fort finally withdrew. All night, during lulls in the conflict, the Volunteers taunted the South Staffs by loudly singing patriotic and rebel songs to show that their morale was high. Not until 9 am on the Saturday was it all over.

TIMELINE
Friday,
28 April

Early morning
The arrival of General Sir John Maxwell from England to take up supreme military command of the British forces in Ireland.

4 pm
The roof of the GPO catches fire.

6 pm
The O'Rahilly is killed in Moore Street while leading a charge against a British barricade.

9 pm
The GPO is a burning ruin. The garrison withdraws to Moore Street.

10 pm – Saturday morning
Bitter fighting in North King Street and at Reilly's Fort.

Early hours of Saturday morning
The murder of fifteen civilian men in North King Street.

Above *British troops stand guard over a barricade at the entrance to the Four Courts at the end of the Rising. The Volunteers from this garrison were involved in the last of the bitter fighting around nearby Reilly's Fort.*

Right *British troops breathe a sigh of relief as they inspect the ruins of the GPO after the rebels' surrender.*

SURRENDER – AND THE AFTERMATH

On Saturday morning, the last pathetic headquarters of the Irish Republic were established in the back parlour of Hanlon's fishmonger's shop at 16 Moore Street. There the decision was taken to surrender. No further retreat was possible without high civilian casualties. It was all over.

One of the three women still with the group, Nurse Elizabeth O'Farrell, made her way up Moore Street wearing Red Cross markings and carrying the white flag of truce. She reached the British barricade at the top of the street, was helped over it and eventually was taken to see General Lowe. He refused to have any dealings with the rebels except to demand an unconditional surrender.

Nurse O'Farrell returned to number 16 and half an hour later returned with Pearse. At 2.30 pm Pearse took off his sword and handed it over to Lowe in the formal act of surrender. Pearse was driven away to see General Maxwell at army headquarters, where he wrote out the formal surrender document. Lowe suggested that Nurse O'Farrell deliver Pearse's surrender order to the other rebel garrisons.

TIMELINE
Saturday, 29 April

9 am
The end of fighting in North King Street.

Mid-morning
The Volunteer leadership decide to surrender.

Noon
Nurse Elizabeth O'Farrell carries the white flag of surrender to the British barrier.

2.30 pm
Patrick Pearse surrenders to Brigadier General Lowe.

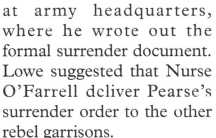

Right Patrick Pearse, in his Volunteer uniform, surrenders to Brigadier General Lowe at the junction of Moore Lane and Parnell Street on Saturday afternoon. On the left is Lowe's son, who served under him.

An eyewitness account of the rebels being marched to Richmond Barracks:

'It's a sight I shall never forget. That thin line, some in the green uniform of the Volunteers, others in the plainer equipment of the Citizen Army, some looking like ordinary civilians, the others looking mere lads of fifteen, not a few wounded and bandaged, and the whole melancholy procession wending its way through long lines of khaki soldiers. But down-hearted – no! As they passed, I heard the subdued strains of the scaffold song of many an Irishman before them – "God Save Ireland".'

Soon after, the injured Connolly was taken to the Red Cross hospital at Dublin Castle, and the main body of Volunteers marched under military orders into Sackville Street, where they laid down their arms before the British. They were soon joined by their colleagues from the Four Courts garrison, the first to receive and act upon the surrender document. There were now about 400 men under arrest. They spent Saturday night in the open, huddled under guard in the gardens of the Rotunda Hospital at the top of Sackville Street.

Captured Volunteers are marched along the north quays by British soldiers and a member of the Royal Irish Constabulary.

At 9 am on Sunday, they were marched off to Richmond Barracks. As the Volunteers passed through some of the poorer areas of the city – areas where many of the men were fighting with the Dublin Fusiliers for the British on the Western Front – they were pelted with rotten fruit and vegetables and had chamber pots emptied over them from high tenement windows.

The leaders were court-martialled. Fifteen of them were sentenced to execution by firing squad, including all the signatories of the proclamation. It was a gruesome business which dragged on from 3 to 12 May. Patrick Pearse, Thomas MacDonagh and Tom Clarke were the first to be shot.

Above After Pearse's surrender in Moore Street, the rebels were marched to Sackville Street, where they gave up their arms. They were held in the grounds of the Rotunda Hospital overnight, then marched to Richmond Barracks.

At first there were few protests, but gradually public opinion began to turn. Many leading figures in Irish public life began to plead for clemency. They were ignored. In the eyes of General Maxwell, a simple soldier, the rebels had committed treason; they had rebelled against lawful authority in the middle of a deadly European war and had consorted with the Germans as well. While most people had expected that the signatories of the Proclamation would be shot, the execution of others was more troubling. There was no consistency: some but not all the deputies were executed; all the garrison commandants were shot – except de Valera. Then, the day after de Valera's reprieve – as people thought that the killings had finished – came the execution that disgusted everyone.

Right Kathleen Clarke (left), in mourning after the execution of her husband, Tom Clarke. Like him, she was an uncompromising republican. Countess Markievicz is at her side.

Father Aloysius, the priest who was with James Connolly till the end, described the execution to Connolly's daughter: *'Such a wonderful man – such a concentration of mind. They carried him in a bed from his ambulance and drove him to Kilmainham Jail. They carried him from the ambulance to the jail yard and put him in a chair . . . He was very brave and cool . . . I said to him, "Will you pray for the men who are about to shoot you?" and he said, "I'll say a prayer for all brave men who do their duty." His prayer was, "Forgive them for they know not what they do," and then they shot him.'*

At dawn on the morning of 12 May, the crippled James Connolly was shot, sitting in a chair. His wife's reaction was that of public opinion at large: 'How could they shoot him? He couldn't sit up in his bed.' And with that, the Easter Rising was over.

The Rising has been described as 'the triumph of failure'. The executions made martyrs of the leaders. As they had hoped and expected, their deaths revived the spirit of republican separatism. The British had wrongly called it the 'Sinn Féin' rebellion, after a small political movement – not even a republican one at that stage – that shared some policies in common with Irish Volunteers but had absolutely nothing to do with the Rising. But the name stuck, and within a year the Sinn Féin party, by then taken over by the republican survivors of the Rising, was winning by-elections.

Sir Roger Casement leaves the Old Bailey during his trial for high treason in the summer of 1916. He was found guilty and was hanged on 3 August.

> *'The truth is that Ireland is not cowed. She is excited a little . . . She was not with the Revolution, but in a few months she will be, and her heart which was withering will be warmed by the knowledge that men have thought her worth dying for.'* – From James Stephens's diary of Easter week.

Rebel prisoners in Richmond Barracks, Dublin, are handed food through the barbed wire by visitors under the watch of British troops. Prisoners were allowed visits from their relatives three times a week.

Another name was born that Easter as well. When Nurse O'Farrell first crossed the barricade in Moore Street prior to the surrender, she said to the first officer she met, 'The commandant of the Irish Republican Army wishes to treat with the commandant of the British forces in Ireland.' The officer replied, 'The Irish Republican Army? The Sinn Féiners, you mean?', to which she said, 'No, the Irish Republican Army they call themselves and I think that is a very good name too.'

TIMELINE

April 1916
The Easter Rising.
May 1916
The execution of the Rising's leaders.
August 1916
Sir Roger Casement is hanged in London for treason.
December 1918
Sinn Féin sweeps nationalist Ireland in the general election.
January 1919
The establishment of an Irish parliament (the *Dail*) by Sinn Féin.
The start of the War of Independence.
December 1920
Ireland is partitioned; the establishment of Northern Ireland.

July 1921
A truce in Southern Ireland between the British and the IRA.
December 1921
The Anglo-Irish Treaty establishes the Irish Free State.
June 1922
The start of the Irish Civil War over the terms of the Anglo-Irish Treaty.
December 1922
The formal establishment of the Irish Free State.
April 1923
The Free State forces are victorious in the Irish Civil War.
June 1949
The Free State becomes the Republic of Ireland.

In 1918, Sinn Féin wiped out the Home Rule Party in the general election. It set up its own parliamentary body in Dublin, refusing to attend the British parliament in Westminster. At the same time, the Irish Republican Army (IRA) began a guerrilla campaign – the War of Independence – to drive the British out by force. Its leader was a brilliant young Corkman, Michael Collins, a veteran of the GPO occupation. By 1922 Sinn Féin and the British had agreed terms for independence in twenty-six of Ireland's thirty-two counties, although the country was partitioned, leaving Northern Ireland – where the majority were in favour of union with Britain – still in the UK.

The Irish Free State, as the new entity was called, was not a republic at first. It finally achieved that status in 1949, although it was in effect independent from 1922. By putting separatism back on the map and making radical republicanism respectable once more in nationalist

Ireland, the Easter Rising proved to be one of the decisive turning points in Irish history.

Had it not happened, we can only say that things would have worked out very differently. The tricolour flag that was so gallantly raised over the GPO that Easter week flies there still today. It is unthinkable that any other flag could ever take its place.

Above *The tricolour flag of the Irish Republic still flies over the GPO in Dublin today. Inside the GPO, in the main hall, stands a statue of the mythical Celtic hero Cuchulain, a memorial to the rebels of 1916.*

Below *The first Dail Eireann (Irish parliament) in 1919 included veterans of the Easter Rising. Among them were Eamon de Valera, Cathal Brugha and Michael Collins, leader of the Irish Republican Army.*

THE FATE OF THE REBELS

Cathal Brugha   Died in the Irish Civil War, six years after the Easter Rising had ended.

Eamonn Ceannt   Executed by firing squad.

Tom Clarke   Executed by firing squad.

James Connolly   Executed by firing squad.

Sean MacDermott   Executed by firing squad.

Thomas MacDonagh   Executed by firing squad. British officers said, '*They all died well, but MacDonagh died like a prince.*'

Countess Constance Markievicz   Condemned to death, but her sentence was commuted to life imprisonment because she was a woman. Released in an amnesty in June 1917, she was the first woman ever elected to the British House of Commons in the general election of 1918; however, she refused to take her seat. She remained a leading figure in Irish radical politics until her death in 1927.

Patrick Pearse   Executed by firing squad.

Joseph Plunkett   Married his fiancée, Grace Gifford, in his cell a few hours before his execution by firing squad.

Eamon de Valera   The only garrison commandant not to be shot after the Rising. He lived until 1975 and became the dominant figure in the politics of independent Ireland. He was *taoiseach* (prime minister) from 1932 to 1948, from 1951 to 1954 and from 1957 to 1959. He was president of Ireland from 1959 to 1973.

GLOSSARY

Boland's Mills An Irish Volunteer garrison on the south-east approach to Dublin, dominating road and rail access to the city.

Curragh A major British army base, situated on a flat heath to the south of Dublin.

Dublin Castle The historic centre of British rule in Ireland.

Fenians Another name for the Irish Republican Brotherhood (IRB). The name comes from the Fianna, a mythical Celtic warrior band.

Four Courts A large building on Dublin's north quays, and the centre of the Irish legal system.

Home Rule The moderate nationalist demand for an Irish domestic parliament within the UK.

IRA The Irish Republican Army, the name adopted by the rebels during the Easter Rising. After independence, the name was kept by the militant minority who rejected the settlement of 1921–22 because it

was not republican enough and because it entailed partition of Ireland.

IRB The Irish Republican Brotherhood. They were extreme militant nationalists, devoted since the 1850s to armed rebellion against Britain. They were the prime movers of the Rising.

Jacob's A large biscuit factory in the south city centre, and one of the rebel strongholds.

Mendicity Institution A centre for the relief of poverty and the dispensing of aid. It was taken over by the rebels as an outpost of the Four Courts command.

Partition The division of Ireland into the Republic of Ireland (the largest area of the island to the south, which became independent) and Northern Ireland (the north-east corner, which remained part of the United Kingdom).

Republic A state that is led by an elected head, rather than a member of a royal family.

Separatism The belief among a group of

people that they should have their own government, instead of being governed from somewhere else.

Sinn Féin A small political group, founded in 1905, which favoured a dual Anglo-Irish monarchy and Irish withdrawal from the British parliament. The British wrongly thought the rebels of the Easter Rising were Sinn Féin. The name was later taken over by the republican political party that arose after the Rising. Sinn Féin is Irish for 'ourselves'.

FURTHER INFORMATION

BOOKS

Biographies

James Connolly: A Political Biography by Austen Morgan
 (Manchester University Press, 1988)

Patrick Pearse: The Triumph of Failure by Ruth Dudley
 Edwards (Gollancz, 1977)

The Easter Rising

The Easter Rebellion by Max Caulfield (Muller, 1964;
 Gill & Macmillan, 1995)

Insurrection in Dublin by James Stephens (C. Smythe,
 1978, 1992)

Histories of Ireland

A Little History of Ireland by Martin Wallace
 (Appletree, 1994)

*Political Violence in Ireland: Government and Resistance
 since 1848* by Charles Townshend (Oxford University
 Press, 1984)

A Short History of Ireland by Richard Killeen (Gill &
 Macmillan, 1994)

Novels

The Informer by Liam O'Flaherty (Jonathan Cape, 1925)

Rebels by Peter de Rosa (Corgi, 1991)

Plays

The Plough and the Stars by Sean O'Casey (French, 1932)

The Shadow of a Gunman by Sean O'Casey (French, 1958)

Short Stories

Collected Stories [two volumes] by Frank O'Connor
 (Pan, 1990)

FILMS

The Informer (1935)

Juno and the Paycock (1930)

The Plough and the Stars (1936)